Sunset

Creative
DRIED FLOWERS

Dried flower arrangements allow you to enjoy the pleasures of a flower-filled house year-round

SUNSET PUBLISHING CORPORATION ■ MENLO PARK, CALIFORNIA

Contents

Published in 1993 by Sunset Publishing Corporation, Menlo Park, CA 94025 by arrangement with J.B. Fairfax Press Pty Limited

First Sunset Printing August 1993

Editor, Sunset Books: Elizabeth L. Hogan

Cover copyright © 1993 Sunset Publishing Corporation
Cover Design by Nina Bookbinder Design; Photography by Bill Zemanek Photography; Photo Styling by Shelley Pennington

Library of Congress Catalog Card Number: 93-84314.
ISBN 0-376-04297-4.
Lithographed in the United States.

J.B. FAIRFAX PRESS PTY LIMITED
EDITORIAL
Managing Editor: Judy Poulos
Editorial Assistant: Ella Martin
Editorial Coordinator: Margaret Kelly
Floral Designs: Sara Waterkeyn, John Lewis, Michelle Porter, Mary Lawrence

PHOTOGRAPHY
Steve Tanner, Steve Lee, Cliff Morgan, Graham Tann, Andrew Elton

DESIGN AND PRODUCTION
Manager: Sheridan Carter
Layout: Lulu Dougherty
Finished Art: Steve Joseph

PRESERVING

Flowers and other growing things are preserved in one of two ways, although there are several different techniques for each method. The first method involves drying the plants with either a combination of air and heat or with a desiccant, such as sand, alum or silica gel, which absorbs moisture from the plant. The other involves preserving the plant material by standing it in diluted glycerine or antifreeze, which the plant absorbs, replacing its own water content. Some flowers are best dried by one method rather than another, but experimenting with different methods can produce interesting results. Eucalyptus leaves, for example, retain their blue-gray color and become brittle when air-dried, but when treated with glycerine, they remain pliable and change to a rich mahogany hue. The preferred method for drying can vary according to the stage of growth of the flower. Hydrangeas in full bloom should be dried with desiccant, while those already starting to dry naturally should be dried with their stems resting in a small amount of water.

AIR-DRYING

Air-drying is very simple and requires no special equipment. Flowers dried in this way can become rather brittle; those dried by being hung upside down can have unnaturally straight stems.

Strawflowers and everlasting flowers – helichrysums, helipterums, and xeranthemums – are most commonly dried in this way. They thrive in hot sunny climates and their paper-thin petals contain very little moisture. Often, they will dry on their own in the garden.

Other suitable plants for decorative arrangements include the seed heads of various common plants and grasses – both wild and ornamental.

Flowers whose heads are made up of many tiny florets, such as baby's breath, lady's mantle and yarrow are also suitable, as are those with petal-like bracts, such as acanthus, or leaf-like calyces, such as Chinese lanterns.

METHOD

The plant material should be dried as quickly as possible, because the longer the process, the more color is lost. Keep the plant warm and well ventilated in a relatively dry environment where it is protected from direct sunlight (which can fade the color of some flowers). Bunches of flowers might look nice hanging up to dry in the kitchen, but the steamy atmosphere is less than ideal.

When drying flowers, strip off all the leaves as soon as possible. Leaves retain moisture and will slow down the drying process; they are also easier to remove cleanly when they are fresh. Dry large flowers individually. Bunches should contain only one type of flower, as the drying times of different flowers vary. Allow the air to circulate freely through and around the bunch and take care not to crush the flowers in the middle.

Drying time depends on the type and moisture content of the plant material and the drying conditions. For a particular plant, the time can also vary from one year to the next, depending on the weather. Completely dry material feels crisp and the stems should snap when bent. To check if the process is complete, stand a sample stem upright for a day or two; if it is still moist, the flower head will droop.

An old-fashioned wooden drying rack which can be raised and lowered is useful for drying flowers and foliage upside down in a high-ceilinged room. You can also use cup hooks, coat hooks or nails, or ordinary clothesline. Chromium-plated rails, free-standing coat racks and hat racks are other possibilities to try.

Chinese lanterns are best dried right-way up from the start, so the lanterns don't end up pointing upwards. Hang the stem on a clothesline, using the uppermost lantern to attach the stem.

The flower heads of many of the everlasting-type flowers – such as xeranthemum and helipterum – are too heavy for the dried stems to support. In these flowers, the stems are usually cut short and the heads are wired, before they are hung to dry.

PRESERVING BY PRESSING

Pressing is as simple as air-drying. In fact, whole branches can be preserved this way, as well as ferns, bracken and spiky leaves. Pressing works best with leaves that are naturally quite flat. It is the one method that retains brilliant autumn leaf color as well as the

5

green of fresh beech. The main drawback is that the end product is two-dimensional and very brittle. Flowers can also be pressed to create dried flower pictures, such as the one on page 79.

METHOD

To dry foliage, carefully arrange the material in a single layer on several pieces of newspaper or blotting paper, making sure that no leaves overlap or curl as they cannot be adjusted once dried. Cover with more layers of newspaper. Apply the necessary pressure by placing the layers under a rug.

You can press individual leaves between the pages of an old telephone directory. For a less flat effect, build the layers up, then leave the "package" somewhere warm and dry – the weight of the pages will do the job. Check the leaves after a week; some may take up to six weeks to dry completely. Store them in the directory until they are needed.

Flowers are best dried in a flower press. See page 17 for how to make and use your own press.

PRESERVING IN A MICROWAVE

This is a newer method which is quite successful with miniature roses or with clusters of small flowers, such as baby's breath, and with grasses. Though the material must still be air-dried afterwards, microwaving speeds up the process and helps to retain the color.

METHOD

Strip away the foliage, then place the flowers or grasses in a single layer on several sheets of paper towel in the microwave oven. Using a medium setting (400-500W), microwave baby's breath for about three minutes and roses for two and a half minutes. Check after three minutes and replace the paper towel if it is soaked. Remove the flowers, then hang them upside down for about three days, as for air-drying. Wipe the microwave oven after each use, as a lot of moisture is released.

PRESERVING IN WATER

Suitable plant material for this method includes fully mature, almost papery, heads of hydrangea; bells-of-Ireland; proteas; and heathers. Yarrow is sometimes dried in this way.

METHOD

Strip off the leaves, then place the flower stem in 1"-2" of water in a warm environment. Do not add more water – it evaporates and is absorbed.

DRYING IN DESICCANTS

This is the least predictable method of preservation. When successful, it produces exquisitely life-like flowers. Unfortunately desiccated flowers are more vulnerable than those preserved by other methods and are best displayed under glass. Suitable flowers include garden roses, zinnias, larkspur, daffodils, dahlias, carnations, marigolds, camellias and pansies. They should all be picked in perfect condition on a dry day, just before they are fully mature.

During desiccation, the water content of the flower is completely absorbed by the surrounding desiccant material. This can be silica gel, borax, alum, sand, or yellow cornmeal or a combination of these. Desiccants vary in weight and in the size of the grains and some are better for certain flowers than others. You can use the desiccant again and again, provided that it is sieved regularly to remove any remaining particles of dried flowers and then dried thoroughly.

Silica gel is the most expensive desiccant, but gives the most reliable results in the shortest time. It is available from floral supply stores in two forms – granular (for more substantial flowers) and powdered (for thin-petalled flowers). The former can take up to three weeks to dry out a plant and the latter perhaps only a day.

Borax and alum are powdery, lightweight and relatively inexpensive, but tend to form lumps when damp. If a petal is slightly wet on the surface, borax and alum sometimes harden and crack. For this reason, borax is sometimes mixed with a rough substance such as cornmeal. Flowers may take a week to dry.

Sand is an old-fashioned desiccant, which needs careful preparation before use. It is relatively heavy, making it unsuitable for many flowers, and takes a long time to dry the flowers thoroughly.

METHOD

Flowers should be cut and placed in the desiccant as soon as possible. Cut the stem to within 1" of the head. The flower can be wired at this point or after drying. Remove any remaining leaves.

The desiccant must be completely dry before you begin. If necessary, spread a thin, even layer of the desiccant in a shallow baking dish and warm it for half an hour in a low oven, 250°. Dry it in the same way after each use.

Put a 1" layer of desiccant in the bottom of a plastic storage box. Gently turn each flower in the desiccant to coat it, then place the flowers in the desiccant, in a single layer and not touching one another. Most flowers dry best if they are placed with their heads up, but larkspur and other spiky flowers should be laid lengthways on the desiccant. Dry one type of flower at a time, as some flowers take longer than others.

Slowly pour a thin stream of desiccant over each flower, so that the space between every petal is filled and the flowers are covered. With open roses, carnations and dahlias, use a toothpick or small paintbrush to separate the petals as you pour. To eliminate air pockets, gently shake or tap the container from time to time.

Cover the flowers with a 1" layer of desiccant; then replace the lid tightly and store in a warm, dry place. The warmer the desiccant, within reason, the quicker the drying and the less the color loss. When the approximate drying time is reached, slowly pour out the desiccant through your hands so you can catch and inspect the first flower. If it feels papery, the flowers are ready to remove; if not, return them to the desiccant for a few days. Flowers left for too long in silica gel become very brittle and dark, but those dried in other desiccants can be stored there without harm.

Any desiccant clinging to the petals can be shaken or brushed off with a fine paintbrush.

PRESERVING WITH GLYCERINE AND ANTIFREEZE

Glycerine, diluted with water, is the traditional method for preserving mature foliage, especially beech and eucalyptus. The glycerine ensures that the material retains its natural shape and flexibility but it is very expensive. Antifreeze, diluted with water, works in much the same way and is less expensive. Take care – they are not always interchangeable; for example, laurel leaves work well with antifreeze but not with glycerine.

Material treated with glycerine or antifreeze lasts indefinitely, and can be dusted or even wiped with a damp cloth without risk.

Unlike air-dried material, which often retains much of its original color, material treated with glycerine and antifreeze changes color completely.

METHOD

Choose only perfect leaves; foliage that is wilted before you start is risky. To help the stems absorb the preservative, strip the bark off and split or crush the bottom 2 inches. Insert the stems into the preservative as soon as possible after cutting.

Dilute the glycerine or antifreeze with hot, or even boiling, water; the harder the stem, the hotter the water should be. Two-thirds water to one-third glycerine or equal parts antifreeze and water is a common ratio. As the glycerine is very thick, mix it thoroughly with water to prevent it from settling.

Choose a narrow container with only 3"-5" of preservative, adding more liquid as it is absorbed. Thick leaves can also be wiped with glycerine occasionally during the preserving process.

Large leaves, such as magnolia, rhododendron, ivy and leather fern, can be preserved individually by submerging them completely in a solution of equal parts glycerine and cold water.

This method of preserving can take from one to six weeks, depending on the size and thickness of the leaves. Some material, such as eucalyptus, is very attractive before it is fully preserved but will not last as long. The process is complete when the foliage feels smooth and has changed color completely, and before drops of preservative appear on the leaf tips or surfaces. Because the preservative is absorbed up the stem, the leaves at the top are the last to be preserved.

PRESERVING THE BRIDAL BOUQUET

Dried flowers bring a touch of nostalgia and never more so than when the flowers are special in themselves. Drying the flowers from your bridal bouquet to keep as a memento of a very special day is a perfect example.

Ideally, the flowers should be dried while they are still at their peak. Refrigerating them until after the honeymoon will not suffice. Leave the bouquet with a friend who can begin drying them for you while you are away.

Take the bouquet apart so the air can circulate around and through the flowers while they hang upside down in a dark spot for three or four weeks. Other drying methods may also be suitable, depending on the type of flowers.

Once the flowers are quite dry, decide how you wish to use them. A heart-shaped wreath is one charming way to arrange the flowers. You can wire or glue the flowers to a purchased wreath base and trim the wreath with trailing satin ribbons.

To dry a complete bouquet, pour borax into a large, deep tin until it is one-third full. Lay the bouquet in the tin and completely cover with borax, making sure the borax goes between the petals. Leave it for about three months.

GROWING FOR DRYING

Statice, strawflowers, and immortelles are fairly easily grown, sun-loving annuals, ideal for preserving. If there is enough space, treat them like a crop and grow them in rows in the vegetable garden where their absence, once they're picked for drying, won't be an eyesore.

Those three everlastings are easy to buy and you may prefer to grow some of the less-familiar annuals for drying. Cockscomb, with its velvety, old-fashioned appeal, is a good choice; there are mixed seeds available with red, yellow, pink, salmon and gold flower heads. Bells-of-Ireland, love-in-a-mist, love-lies-bleeding and zinnias, if you are prepared to preserve them in a desiccant, are other good choices. Seed mixtures with differing growth rates are also available. Whichever flowers you choose, a good seed bed is essential. Use very little fertilizer; too much foliage growth will inhibit the lush growth of flowers.

Preserved foliage is especially difficult to buy, and the raw material is quite easy to grow, even in the shadiest garden or in a pot.

Seed pods are also valuable as dried material, as the pleasure of the flowering period in the garden is not cut short. The flowers of popular dried pods such as Chinese lantern and money plant are insignificant, and their only decorative value in the garden is in the pod stage.

HARVESTING

There are a few general rules about harvesting:

☐ Always harvest on a dry day, as morning dew or rain clinging to the flowers and foliage can cause rot.

☐ Always harvest during warm, dry, sunny weather.

☐ Be aware of impending local frosts and avoid growing plants for drying in known frost pockets, areas exposed to high winds or to early morning mists.

☐ Preserving inferior, damaged or discolored material is a waste of time.

☐ Some plants can be picked at various stages in their development. Wild grasses, for example, can be picked while in flower and yellow with pollen or when fully ripe and turning gold.

☐ For flowers with one optimum moment for harvesting, it is usually just before the flowers are fully open and before the color fades.

Harvest fluffy material, such as clematis and pampas grass, when the seed pods are hairy but not yet fluffy. They continue to ripen and become fluffy as they dry. An aerosol fixative, such as hair spray, can help prevent very fragile and delicate seed heads shattering.

Foliage preserved with glycerine or antifreeze needs to be mature; young green foliage will not absorb the solution adequately. Autumn is usually too late because the solution will not be drawn up through the stems.

WILD PLANTS

Some plants are protected by law and local authorities can supply a list. You must also seek permission from the landowner, before entering to search for suitable plants. Use a pair of clippers or pruning shears when collecting, for a quick, clean cut. Pulling up plants is unnecessary and very destructive, and against all environmental preservation principles.

Because some time can elapse between collecting wild flowers and starting the drying process, place delicate specimens in a sealed plastic bag. Don't leave them in the bag indefinitely or they may rot.

Below: Flowers for drying should be picked at their peak

Tree and shrub branches are indispensable for large-scale arrangements, especially those with colored bark, such as redtwig dogwood, or an elegant shape, such as hazel or birch.

Dried sweet-smelling ingredients for potpourri

Grow fresh herbs to make this wonderful scented wreath

BUYING DRIED FLOWERS

Dried flowers are available from many florists, craft shops, supermarkets, department stores and garden centers. These days, even some home furnishing shops sell bunches of dried flowers to coordinate with their new fabrics each season. In addition, there are shops specializing in dried flowers. Such shops are a treasure trove of interesting materials and useful information. Wherever you buy, follow these simple rules:

☐ Buy dried flowers from a shop with a rapid turnover of stock, to avoid old material.

☐ Dried flowers should not be displayed in direct sunlight, which will fade colors, and, to avoid crushing, should not be squashed together.

☐ Look for strong natural color.

☐ Check for broken stems or missing flower heads. Gently pull back the cellophane and give a very gentle shake to see if the flower heads are secure. A gentle tap or shake should reveal any brittle flowers and seed heads harvested when over-mature.

☐ Check large seed heads for splits and cracks.

☐ Check for signs of mold on the stem.

☐ The tiny flowers of baby's breath and broom often fall off, but because the stems are tightly massed in a bunch, it can be hard to tell how many sprigs are flowerless. Compare two or three bunches and pick the fullest.

☐ Check that pre-mixed bunches are not made up of leftovers with varying lengths of stems.

BUYING FRESH FLOWERS

If you don't have a garden, you can buy fresh flowers and dry them. Ask the florist for the freshest possible material in perfect condition, not flowers that have been in cold storage for some time, as these have a high water content and are difficult to dry. It is also a good idea to buy from a florist with a quick turnover of stock; the flowers are more likely to be fresh.

OTHER MATERIALS

Non-floral materials can add a new dimension to your arrangements. Here is a list of some of the most common types used, but you should use whatever gives you the effect you want.

CONES

Pine cones have always been popular, especially at Christmas time, when they are often spray-painted gold or silver. Cones in their natural state, such as the ones on page 74, can be very effective year-round. Cones vary a great deal in size and some, such as the spruce cones, vary in color as well.

GOURDS

Gourds, in various shapes and sizes, are an inexpensive source of color and body in an arrangement. They can be grown from seed. Varnishing a thoroughly dried gourd with a clear polyurethane will give it an attractive glossy look and help to preserve it at the same time.

MOSS

Moss is widely used as a "ground" or surface cover, to conceal florist's foam and add a natural effect. If you are lucky enough to be able to collect your own moss, take care removing the soil, then dry the moss in a warm room. You can buy sphagnum moss (soft and low), Spanish moss (natural gray or dyed green), and deer moss (to the left of the raffia and white ribbon).

NUTS

Most nuts can be used, either in their natural state, sprayed with a clear gloss or gold or silver. The easiest way to attach nuts is with glue, if that is possible. If it is not possible, drill a small hole in each nut and then wire it in the usual way.

PAINTS

Whether you paint your dried flowers or not is largely a matter of personal taste. Many people choose to spray paint the container or basket but not the flowers. Spray paints are quick and easy to use but do not allow you very much control. Brush painting, with poster paints or water-based colors, gives you more control and produces more subtle effects. You can also achieve interesting changes in the color of cones with bleaching.

A final coat of clear polyurethane varnish will enrich the natural colors and add gloss.

RAFFIA
Available from craft shops, raffia can be used in many ways. It can form the base of an arrangement, such as a swag or wreath, or can be used as a decorative feature.

RIBBONS
The right ribbon can add the perfect finishing touch. Choose one that complements your arrangement, not only in color but also in style and finish. A shiny, satin ribbon may not suit a harvest-type arrangement. Whichever one you choose, always cut the ends at an angle, not straight across.

STONES
Pebbles and stones can be used to camouflage stems in glass containers or to add weight to a container to prevent it from toppling. A great variety of stones can be bought from gardeners' and builders' supply stores. You can also buy small quantities of gravel from stores selling tropical fish and aquarium supplies.

Left: A great variety of non-floral materials can be used to supplement dried flowers in arrangements
Above: Combine a variety of non-plant materials for special effects

15

TOOLS AND EQUIPMENT

DROP CLOTHS

Working with dried flowers, particularly in a large arrangement, can make quite a mess. Laying down a drop cloth is a good idea to protect your surroundings.

FLORISTS' FOAM

Gray or brown florists' foam (also known as sahara) is generally used for dried flowers and the green variety (oasis) for fresh ones. Both are available in blocks and various shapes, such as balls and cones. The advantage of foam is that stems remain exactly where you put them. Polystyrene performs the same function and is cheaper but breaks up more easily.

FLORISTS' STEM TAPE

This plastic tape, which comes in a variety of colors including green, brown and white, is used for binding stems, particularly where there is wire to be concealed. Store the rolls of tape in a cool dry place, as the tape will be difficult to work with if it is not kept cool.

FROGS

Plastic frogs or florists' spikes are useful for anchoring the foam to the bottom of the container with "stickum" (see below). As an inexpensive alternative, make your own by pressing two floral pins into a base of stickum.

GLUE

A clear, quick-drying glue or epoxy is essential for securing ribbons or attaching plant material to the arrangement. A hot glue gun is ideal for this purpose.

KNIFE

A sharp craft knife is useful for cutting and sharpening stems, and shaping foam blocks.

"STICKUM"

Stickum is an adhesive generally sold in a roll at florists' and craft shops. It is useful for anchoring material to the clean, dry surface of the container.

WIRE

Steel wire, usually called florists' wire, sold on a spool or cut into short lengths, is essential for working with dried flowers. The thickness of a wire can be described in millimeters or by its gauge. The higher the gauge number, the thinner the wire.

Annealed spool wire, most often used for joining flower stems into bunches or for attaching moss to a wreath base, comes in several thicknesses. The one most commonly used is 24 gauge. 28 gauge wire, silver colored or painted green and more commonly called spool wire, is thinner and is used for more delicate work, such as

wiring individual florets. Spool wire can be cut with scissors to any length.

Long, straight wires, called stub wires, are available in various lengths and thicknesses. For most work with dried flowers, 24 gauge or 22 gauge is suitable.

Floral pins, bent wires that look like wires bent in U-shapes, are useful for attaching moss and for making wreaths and balls.

Store wires in a container in a dry place to protect them from rusting. Separate different lengths and thicknesses into different containers for ease of working.

CHICKEN WIRE

Galvanized wire hexagonal mesh ($^1/_2$"-1") forms a base for many floral arrangements in this book. If you cannot locate $^1/_2$" mesh in a manageable amount, substitute florists' foam as a base for container arrangements. Chicken wire is handy for strengthening foam in large arrangements, or for controlling a shape, like the moss "wall" on page 64.

WIRE CUTTERS, SCISSORS AND CLIPPERS

You will need some efficient cutting equipment, but not necessarily all three of these types. A good pair of kitchen shears that cut wire will do very well.

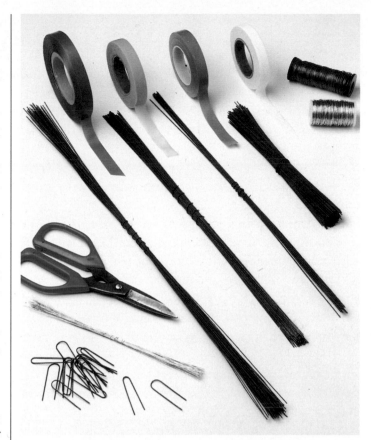

Far left and above: A selection of tools and equipment used for working with dried flowers

MAKING A FLOWER PRESS

You will need:
- [ ] 2 pieces of $^1/_2$" thick plywood, each 7" x 7"
- [ ] 4 bolts, 2" long, and 4 washers
- [ ] 4 wing nuts
- [ ] thick cardboard
- [ ] sheets of blotting paper

INSTRUCTIONS

1 Round off the corners of both pieces of plywood. Paint them at this point, stencilling or painting a finishing decoration if you wish. Allow to dry.

2 Mark the holes at each corner of the plywood pieces for the bolts, taking care that the holes on the top and bottom piece are aligned. Drill the holes.

3 Cut several sheets of cardboard and blotting paper into 7" squares, cutting off the corners to allow for the bolts.

4 Insert the bolts through the bottom piece of plywood first. Lay a sheet of cardboard and another two sheets of blotting paper on top and so on until the press is full. Place

the top plywood piece in place and secure it with the washers and wing nuts.

To use your flower press, place the flowers between the sheets of blotting paper, assembling layers of cardboard, blotting paper, flowers, blotting paper and cardboard. Once the press is full, tighten the nuts and leave the flower press in a cool, dry place for about three weeks. When the flowers are papery dry to the touch, they are ready to remove from the press.

WIRING METHODS

Dried flowers are generally wired in order to replace weak stems with a stem that is both strong and flexible. Wiring is also used to make small bunches to accentuate the color. Natural stems held together do not give the same effect, as the flower heads tend to push outwards.

To wire bunches, choose two or three sprigs of flowers with stems of a similar length. Take a length of wire approximately twice the length of the stem and bend it in the middle so that one half is at right angles to the other. Place the wire along the stem with the bend just under the flower heads or seed pods. Twist the outward facing leg of wire round and round the stem and the other leg of the wire. Secure it well at the bottom and pinch the two legs together at the top.

Wire can be used also to extend the natural stem, as

with the purple statice pictured. The bending and wrapping method is the same but the wire used must be longer.

Everlastings are probably the most commonly wired flowers, because the natural stems tend to be thick and not very attractive, and the heads can droop. (In tightly packed arrangements this is not a problem, because the stems are hidden and the massed flower heads support one another.) To wire them, push a length of wire up through the center of the flower and

make a small hook at the top. Pull down on the wire, pulling the hook into the flower head. It is easier to wire the flower heads before drying, but rust stains can result, especially on pale-colored flowers. Dry flower heads may be more difficult to wire. The solution is to dry the flowers for a week, wire them, then leave them to continue the drying process.

Wired stems can be covered with florists' tape or arranged in such a way that the wire is not visible. It is also possible to insert the wire into the hollow stem of some flowers, such as larkspur.

To use the taping method, begin by securing the tape just under the flower head with two or three turns of the tape. Continue working down the stem, winding the tape diagonally, overlapping the edges as you go.

Pine cones can be wired by bending a length of wire into a U-shape so that it fits neatly within one ring of scales at the lower end, then twisting the ends of the wire together. You won't need to tape the wires unless they are visible.

Far left: Wire small bunches of flowers before use
Left: Wired flowers
Above: Small flowers may need to be wired but flowers and leaves with strong stems do not

CONTAINERS

The right container can be the making of a dried flower arrangement. It should be complementary to the flowers used in shape, size and color. It should also suit the room in which the arrangement is to be displayed. An exact color-match is rarely a consideration because flowers do not have a single flat color, but have a color variation throughout the flower.

It is more important that the container suits the arrangement in "feeling" – a simple one for a simple arrangement and a more sophisticated one for a sophisticated arrangement. Occasionally a contrast of style works well, but this is not always easy to achieve.

Sometimes, it is the container which dictates the style of the arrangement. The lovely china jug decorated with painted roses on page 27 cries out for old-fashioned, feminine flowers, while the old rusting watering can shown here lends itself to a more casual, country look. This is not to say that an absolutely literal translation of the container into the flowers will always work as well. Experiment with a variety of flowers and containers.

Because dried flowers do not need water, you can use a large number of containers that would not be suitable for fresh flower arrangements, such as baskets. Terracotta pots are wonderful for informal groupings of flowers and grasses, as well as being ideally suited for topiary or standards. Pieces of bark, decorative items like picture frames, bed posts and sea shells and even straw hats, marry well with arrangements of dried flowers.

Remember, it is the water which adds the "ballast" to a large flower arrangement, preventing it from toppling over. In the absence of water, you will need to provide this weight in other ways: with sand, pebbles, marbles or gravel.

The nature of dried flowers means that they do not have the natural curve of fresh flowers and stems; the arrangements can look very stiff and upright. This effect can be softened by the choice of the right container, such as an open-weave basket, which allows you to insert stems between the weave.

Sometimes, the neck of a container can be too narrow, forcing all the stems to stand tightly together. Inserting a ball of florists' foam into the neck, so that it

protrudes from the top, allows the stems to be pushed in at various angles and to droop downwards as well. If the neck is really narrow, you can secure the foam to the top of the container with stickum and tape.

Clear glass containers can be a problem, because the stems of the flowers are clearly visible through the glass. If you can line the container with moss, as has been done with the one on page 22, the effect is quite pleasing. Many other materials, such as sand, marbles, potpourri and gravel, can also serve as a lining. If your glass container is not a precious one, you can actually glue the lining to the inside of the glass or even glue fabric or paper to the outside.

Left and above: You can use just about anything you please as a container for your dried flowers. Make sure that the size and appearance of the container complement your arrangement

CARING FOR DRIED FLOWERS

The enemies of dried flowers are:
- ☐ accidental damage
- ☐ moisture, leading to mildew
- ☐ dust
- ☐ fluctuations in temperature, resulting in condensation
- ☐ overcrowding
- ☐ direct, strong light

STORAGE

Dried plant material is best stored in long, relatively shallow, cardboard boxes. Make certain there are holes which allow the air to enter and circulate around the contents. Wrap bunches of like flowers in tissue or newspaper, and lay the bunches in a "head and foot" arrangement in the box. Adding a small packet of desiccant to the bottom of the box is a good idea, as there is almost certain to be residual moisture. Never wrap dried plant material in plastic.

Label each box clearly with its contents and store the box in a dry place that is not subject to great temperature variations.

Very delicate material can be stored hanging upside down in a protected spot. An umbrella of tissue paper will help to protect it from light and dust. The most delicate are the desiccated flowers; they need to be stored "standing up" in airtight bins with crumpled tissue around the stems.

Small arrangements can be successfully stored in a box with crumpled paper around them, and either a lid or an umbrella of paper taped over the top. Large arrangements may need to be dismantled and stored as described for loose flowers.

CLEANING

A soft brush can be used to dust the more rigid dried materials. Leaves which have been dried with glycerine can be wiped clean with a damp cloth, restoring their shine.

RECYCLING

Unlike fresh flowers, dried flowers do not signal the end of their life with brown, droopy heads and smelly stems. Their color may fade, but many find this change quite pleasing. You can recycle the flowers from an old arrangement quite simply, sometimes adding in a few new pieces for effect. If your old arrangement is a long-stemmed one, you might cut the stems quite short for a densely packed low arrangement in a different container.

Removing any damaged material, changing the container and rearranging the contents are other ways of recycling. A big arrangement might make two or three small, pretty ones.

It is possible to make minor repairs before you recycle. A rose can be reshaped by steaming it over a kettle for a few minutes, then gently re-forming it. Petals which have broken away can be reattached with a dot of white glue that dries clear.

Use a soft brush to dust the arrangement

22

SCIENTIFIC CLASSIFICATION

Wherever possible, common names for plants and flowers have been used throughout this book. The following table gives the common name and botanical-name equivalent (in Latin) for the flowers or plants mentioned. Some common names refer to one specific plant; others apply to a number of related species.

COMMON NAME	LATIN NAME	COMMON NAME	LATIN NAME
Baby's breath	*Gypsophila elegans* and *G. paniculata*	Lavender	*Lavandula* species
		Lotus	*Nelumbo* species
Barley	*Hordeum* species	Love-in-a-mist	*Nigella damascena*
Bells-of-Ireland	*Moluccella laevis*	Love-lies-bleeding	*Amaranthus caudatus*
Broom	*Cytisus* species, *Genista* species	Oats, wild	*Avena fatua*
Canary grass	*Phalaris canariensis*	Poppy	*Papaver* species
Chinese lantern	*Phydsalis alkekengi*	Protea	*Protea* species
Cockscomb	*Celosia cristata*	Rat's tail statice	*Psylliostachys suworowii*
Everlasting flowers	*Helichrysum* (several species)	Reed grass	*Phalaria arundinacea*
		Rosy sunray	*Acroclinium roseum*
Globe thistle	*Echinops* species	Sea holly	*Eryngium* species
Goldenrod	*Solidago* species	Sea lavender	*Limonium* species
Hare's- or rabbit-tail grass	*Lagarus ovatus*	Strawflower	*Helichrysum bracteatum*
Honesty or Money plant	*Lunaria* species		
Hydrangea	*Hydrangea* species	Swan River everlasting	*Helipterum manglesii*
Immortelle	*Xeranthemum annuum*	Tartarian statice	*Goniolimon tataricum*
Lady's mantle	*Alchemilla mollis*	Teasel	*Dipsacus sylvestris*
Larkspur	*Consolida ambigua*	Yarrow	*Achillea* species

1 *Helichrysum bracteatum (Strawflower)* This pretty flower is one of the most commonly used in dried flower arrangements. It is best harvested when in full bloom, before the yellow center becomes too visible. Air-dry.

2 *Acroclinium roseum (Rosy sunray)* Harvest this flower, also called everlasting flower, when it is in mid-to-full bloom. Air-dry.

3 *Rosa (Rose)* Roses should be dried when the flower heads are still quite tight. They may be air-dried or dried by submerging in a desiccant, such as borax. Make sure the desiccant reaches into all parts of the flower.

4 *Helichrysum (Everlasting flower)* See no. 1.

5 *Achillea (Yarrow)* Pick in its bloom, before the head is fully open and the color begins to fade. Air-dry.

6 *Xeranthemum annuum (Immortelle)* Pick this flower in mid- to full- bloom and air-dry.

7 *Limonium sinuatum (Statice)* Another very popular flower for drying, this flower is best picked in mid- to full-bloom and air-dried.

8 *Consolida ambigua (Larkspur)* Much prized for its lovely color, this flower should be harvested before the seeds turn brown and split apart.

9 *Lavandula (Lavender)* The most traditional flower for drying, prized for its lovely scent, lavender should be picked in mid- to prime-bloom and air-dried.

10 *Goniolimon tataricum (Tartarian statice)* See no. 7.

11 *Hydrangea* Collect these blooms for drying as the petals start to feel papery. Air-dry.

24

12 *Solidago (Goldenrod)* Wonderful for adding bulk to a display, this flower should be collected in its prime. Air-dry.

13 *Physalis alkekengi (Chinese lantern)* Pick at the orange, pod stage, before the color begins to fade. Air-dry.

14 *Papaver (Poppy seedheads)* Harvest the green seed pods before they split. Air-dry.

15 *Amaranthus candatus (Love-lies-bleeding)* Also growing in a globe form, this flower is best picked before the color changes. Air-dry.

16 *Lagurus ovatus (Hare's- or rabbit-tail grass)* For green tails, pick after flowering or a little later for more silvery colored ones. Air-dry.

17 *Lunaria annua (Honesty)* Most commonly, this is picked at the mature stage when the silver center is exposed. Air-dry.

18 *Phaliaris canariensis (Canary grass)* Harvest after flowering when the tops are a good green color and not yet changing color. Air-dry.

19 *Hordeum (Barley)* Pick this dramatic grain when the heads are fully formed and before they bend. Air-dry.

20 *Avena fatua (Wild oats)* Harvest the stems when the green ears are fully formed. Air-dry.

Table Arrangements

Whether in a basket, a vase or an old rusty watering can, an arrangement of dried flowers on your table or dresser will be a constant source of pleasure. The style of the arrangement is largely a matter of individual taste and your home decor but, when you consider the variety of containers and flowers available, the possibilities are almost endless.

A book of flower arrangements can be a very frustrating thing, prescribing a particular collection of flowers to be arranged in a certain container or vase. Your greatest pleasure will come from being able to adapt an idea to suit your own flowers and vase.

The charming arrangement pictured opposite is quite informal, lending itself to various groupings of cottage garden flowers, depending on what you have available. Take care only to retain the general shape and proportion of the arrangement. The china jug and wash basin not only provide the container, but also define your color scheme. If you can manage it, using flowers that are pictured on the jug is a lovely touch.

The colors of the china pattern are reflected in the sea lavender, everlastings, love-in-a-mist, white larkspur and myrtle foliage.

To achieve the shape, wedge a block of florists' foam into the opening of the jug. Begin by placing the taller, upright stems in the center, then fill in the shorter stems, gradually opening out the triangular shape towards the base. Angle the lower stems slightly downwards, covering the top of the jug.

A DAY IN THE COUNTRY

MATERIALS
suitable basket
chicken wire
21 gauge spool wire
blue larkspur
baby's breath
love-in-a-mist
pink and yellow everlasting flowers
hydrangeas

INSTRUCTIONS

1 Cover the top of the basket with chicken wire, using the spool wire to attach the chicken wire to the sides of the basket.

2 Begin to build up the outline, using tall stems of larkspur or something similar in form, if the larkspur is unavailable.

3 Fill in the shape, using fluffy, white baby's breath and clumps of flowering love-in-a-mist, positioning them lower down in the basket and keeping them well scattered.

Above: Begin to form the arrangement with tall stems of larkspur
Right: The finished arrangement

An old bicycle basket makes a perfect container for this delightfully random display of dried flowers. The arrangement features a gentle blending of lavender blue, pink and white. For a bright and casual look, choose red, yellow and orange flowers.

4 The focal flowers in the display are the pretty pink and yellow everlasting flowers. Place large clumps of them throughout the arrangement, making sure the heads stand out well. It is not a good idea to place these tiny flowers individually in this particular arrangement, as the charming country look is best achieved with clumps of flowers.

5 Finish off the basket with a ring of dried hydrangeas tucked in around the rim. This helps to lift the other flowers and forms an effective link between the basket and the display.

Take care to arrange the everlasting flowers so that the heads stand out

FIELD SONG

MATERIALS
suitable basket
chicken wire, formed into a ball
24 gauge wire
clumps of wild oats
bunches of love-in-a-mist
small and large poppy seedheads
clumps of sea holly
large globe thistle heads
various grasses
lotus pods

INSTRUCTIONS

1 Attach the ball of chicken wire into the taller end of the basket and secure with wire.

2 Arrange several clumps of oats with their ends in the chicken wire ball. Cut the lengths so that the long ones overhang the lower lip of the basket, with the clumps becoming shorter and more upright towards the back.

3 Intersperse the oats with wired bunches of love-in-a-mist, maintaining the general shape, with the longer, low-lying stems at the front and the shorter upright ones at the back.

First arrange the clumps of oats in the basket

4 Add in bunches of small poppy seedheads, arranged mainly towards the front so that they appear to be spilling over the lip of the basket. Place a few large poppy seedheads here and there, for contrast.

5 Arrange clumps of sea holly throughout the arrangement. They add an interesting blue highlight to the otherwise neutral tones. If you cannot get any sea holly, choose a similar plant to give that colored highlight. Concentrate these around the handle, pushing them deep into the arrangement, and then place a few long stems in the foreground. Remember, with each element you add, the idea is to maintain the general shape.

6 Soften the whole arrangement by adding a few grasses, and then place several lotus pods at the back, using them to cover any exposed chicken wire.

You don't need a large variety of colored flowers to make a pleasing display. Choose a basket with a slightly lower lip on one end to help you define the shape of the arrangement.

Left: Add some small poppy seedheads

Arrange clumps of sea holly and large globe thistle heads

Add grasses and seedheads to complete the arrangement

Field Song (see page 31)

Sweet Lavender

Make this delightful potpourri basket in two very different styles. The first is a dramatic arrangement of lavender with highlights of red everlasting flowers. The second is the picture of femininity, tied up with lilac tulle.

MATERIALS

small lined basket
18 or 24 gauge stub wire
lavender
small red everlasting flowers
³/₄ yd red satin ribbon
fine spool wire
potpourri

INSTRUCTIONS

1 Wire the lavender into small bunches, each containing three or four stems. Attach one of the bunches to the rim of the basket by wiring through the wicker work. Attach a second bunch of lavender with the flower heads overlapping the stems of the first bunch. Continue working in this way until the entire rim of the basket is covered.

2 When the rim is complete, cover the handle of the basket in the same way.

3 Wire the everlasting flowers into bunches of five or six flowers each. Attach these bunches at intervals around the rim of the basket and on the handle.

4 Make a bow from the red satin ribbon and wire it to the center of the handle. Cover the wire with a stem of lavender, fixed in place with the fine spool wire.

5 Fill the basket with your choice of potpourri. Select one that complements the colors and scent of the arrangement.

The complete arrangement with its lavender-covered handle

34

LILAC TIME

MATERIALS
small lined basket
18 or 24 gauge stub wire
red love-lies-bleeding
blue larkspur
soft pink everlasting flowers
1½ yds lilac tulle trim, 6" wide
potpourri

INSTRUCTIONS

1 Wire small stems of love-lies-bleeding into clumps. Attach these to the rim of the basket with wire. Keep the angles irregular so that some stems are standing up and some are hanging down.

2 Fill in between the love-lies-bleeding with wired clumps of blue larkspur and pink everlasting flowers, forming a dense ring of flowers around the rim of the basket.

3 Cut the lilac tulle trim into three lengths, each approximately 18" long. Tie the strips into bows. Wire a bow to each end of the handle and one to the center of the handle. Open out the tulle to give a full appearance to the bows.

4 Fill the basket with potpourri, choosing one that complements the color and scent of the arrangement. Refresh your potpourri from time to time with small amounts of essential oils.

The finished basket trimmed with bows of lilac tulle

Bring a touch of country charm into your living room with this beautiful arrangement of garden flowers. We have used a small wicker shopping basket which looks charming just as it is. If you prefer a more formal look, spray-paint the basket in a color to coordinate with the flowers.

Roses and Lace (see page 38)

ROSES AND LACE

MATERIALS
small basket with handle
chicken wire
18 or 24 gauge stub wire
sea lavender
love-in-a-mist
soft pink larkspur
lady's mantle
roses

INSTRUCTIONS

1 Wire the sea lavender, love-in-a-mist, larkspur and lady's mantle into bunches and each rose individually.

4 Insert wired clumps of love-in-a-mist into the arrangement so they stand out above the the sea lavender.

5 Fill in with bunches of pink larkspur. Try not to obscure the handle completely, but have the arrangement slightly parted at the handle.

6 Finally, add the bunches of lady's mantle and several roses to complete the soft romantic picture.

2 Cover the top of the basket with the chicken wire, attaching it to the rim of the basket by wiring through the wicker work.

3 Form a base for the arrangement by packing the chicken wire with clumps of sea lavender.

Top: Begin with wired bunches of love-in-a-mist
Center: Filling out the arrangement
Right: Adding the finishing touches

BOUNTIFUL

MATERIALS

china jug
spool wire
fresh damp moss
chicken wire
blue everlasting flowers
yarrow in two colors, blue and pearl
18 or 24 gauge stub wire
oats

INSTRUCTIONS

1 Begin by making a garland of flowers to fit around the neck of the jug. There are two ways to do this: you can wire the flower stems together to form the garland, or you can wrap moss with wire using this as a base for the flowers. For the latter method, take some fresh, damp moss and roll it into a cylindrical shape. Don't make it too thick as the flowers will add a lot of bulk when they are attached. Starting at one end, bind the moss tightly with spool wire, keeping the turns quite close together, and leaving a long tail of wire at each end. Cut off any loose bits of moss as you go. Allow the moss to dry.

2 Mold a piece of chicken wire into a ball and place it inside the jug.

Dress up your hallway with a beautiful old china jug, bursting with sheaves of oats. This is an ideal arrangement for those tight corners or narrow spaces, because it spreads upwards rather than outwards.

Above: Preparing the moss ring
Left: Insert a ball of chicken wire into the jug

3 Wrap the moss frame around the neck of the jug and secure it in place by twisting the tails of wire together.

4 Wire the flowers into small bunches and insert them into the moss frame. Push the wires in at a slight angle so the flowers lie close to the moss rather than sticking out at right angles. Arrange the different flowers alternately around the moss frame, packing them close together to form a thick ring of flowers around the neck of the jug.

5 Cut a large amount of oat stalks to the same length and wire them into small bundles. Push one bundle at a time into the wire mesh inside the jug. Make sure they are packed tightly and stand up straight.

Top: Secure the frame with the loose wire
Left: Push the wired flowers into place
Below: Use generous quantities of oats for a dramatic effect
Right: The finished arrangement

Choose flowers that complement the color and design of your jug as these pretty blue and cream ones do. You could opt for more contrasting colors if you prefer.

YESTERYEAR

The right container is crucial to the success of your dried flower arrangement – often it is the most unlikely container that works best. In this case, a battered old metal watering can has been given a new lease on life as part of an imaginative arrangement of flowers, grains and grasses. Tag sales and flea markets are a great source of materials and inspiration.

MATERIALS
suitable container
chicken wire
barley
purple immortelles
yellow-dyed hare's- or rabbit-tail grass
brown knife acacia (Acacia cultriformis)
raffia

INSTRUCTIONS

1 Roll the chicken wire into a cylinder and pack the mesh into the neck of the watering can.

2 Build up the shape of the arrangement with tall bundles of barley. You do not need to wire the stalks; simply gather them into small bundles and place them in the chicken wire, on both sides of the handle.

3 Scatter purple immortelles in between the stalks of barley. Vary the height of the immortelles stems, cutting some quite short and keeping others as tall as the barley stalks.

4 Continue to fill out the shape of the arrangement, using plenty of the yellow-dyed hare's- or rabbit-tail grass. Add the stems of grass one by one and concentrate them around the base to conceal the top of the watering can.

5 Add depth to your display with long stems of brown knife acacia, taking care to maintain the general outline of the arrangement.

6 Push a few stems of purple immortelles and barley into the spout so they look as though they are spilling out.

Top: Begin by packing the neck of the watering can with chicken wire
Right: The barley adds an interesting color contrast

7 As a finishing touch, make a raffia bow. Cut your raffia into three slim bundles of equal length, retaining a few strands for tying. Tie the bundles together securely at one end, braid them and tie the other end with another strand of raffia. Tie the braid into a simple bow, and then tie the bow to the handle of the watering can. If you prefer, you can use fabric or paper ribbon for the bow.

The completed arrangement with its raffia bow

COTTAGE HEDGE

This is a charming arrangement which features lovely, old-fashioned flowers arranged in a very contemporary way. It utilizes an interesting way of grouping the flowers by height.

MATERIALS
small rectangular basket
floral foam
glue gun
10-12 roses
10-12 stems larkspur
statice
hydrangeas
paper twist ribbon for the bow
*¹/₄" wide satin ribbon for the
    tiny bow*

INSTRUCTIONS

1 Cut the foam to fit the basket, and glue it in place on the bottom of the basket.

2 Carefully cut the rose stems so they are all exactly the same length. Center the roses in a line in the middle of the foam.

3 Trim the larkspur, statice and hydrangeas so that each bunch has stems the same length. Place them in the foam around the roses, first the larkspur, then the statice and finally the hydrangeas. Make sure that the hydrangeas fill out the bottom of the arrangement, covering the lip of the basket, hiding the foam and spilling over the edge of the basket.

4 Make a bow from the paper twist ribbon and glue it to the center front of the basket. Tie a tiny bow from the satin ribbon and glue it to the center of the paper bow.

This pretty arrangement is from Michele Porter of Artistic Pursuits.

This is quite a small arrangement, but you could easily adopt the same principles for a much larger basket.

Hanging Decorations

Dried flower arrangements, hung on walls, over windows or suspended from the ceiling, open up a whole new world of decorating possibilities. They can be as ornate as you wish or as simple as a bunch of flowers hung from the ceiling.

Wreaths, formerly seen only at Christmas time, are becoming more and more popular year-round. Wreaths for special occasions, such as birthdays or anniversaries, are a great idea. Drying the flowers of a bridal bouquet and forming them into a wreath makes a charming memento for a bride.

The wreath shown here is made from lichen-covered pine branches that have been twisted over a wire base. As an alternative to pine, any flexible branches or vines will do and the latter probably will not require any base at all. Prunings of grape or young willow are ideal.

There are three general ways in which you can attach the trimmings to your wreath: gluing, wiring or weaving. In this wreath the everlasting flowers have been wired and woven in as the base was formed, fuller at the bottom and diminishing towards the top so the interesting features of the base can still be seen. If you are working on a prepared base, the preferred method is to wire the trimmings, either individually or in small bunches, and then wire or glue them into the base.

Experiment with trimmings, adding ribbons, seed pods and purchased decorations. It is a good idea to have a fairly clear plan for your wreath before you begin; laying it out on the table to work out the balance of shape and color before you begin is a good idea. Don't forget to add a wire loop to the back for hanging your wreath.

HEART'S DESIRE

MATERIALS
dry, flexible twigs (silver birch or
*   willow are ideal)*
18 gauge stub wire
scissors
1½ yds of 1" wide satin ribbon
craft glue
baby's breath
miniature roses

INSTRUCTIONS

1 Choose twigs which are flexible enough to bend into the shape you want without breaking. Trim off any rough ends and cut the twigs into 24" lengths. Divide the bunch of twigs into two halves.

2 Place the two bundles of twigs together with the ends even. Wind wire around one end of the bundle. Wind another length of wire around the bundle about 8" further along. Separate the two bundles at

Right: The completed arrangement
Below: Forming the heart-shaped wreath

This beautiful heart-shaped decoration is perfect for Valentine's Day. Its simple form is offset by the sprays of baby's breath, miniature roses and lavish satin bows.

Cover the wire with satin ribbon

twigs together at that point. Cover these wired sections with a length of satin ribbon, placing the join in the ribbon at the back of the wreath. Leaving a tail of wire to push into the wreath, wind wire around one end of the ribbon before wrapping it around the twigs. The wire will serve to hold the wrap in place, or you can glue the ribbon in place, if you prefer.

5 Make two bows from the ribbon, secure them with wire through the center, and glue or wire them to the ribbon-wrapped sections on either side of the wreath. Attach a length of wired ribbon to the top of the wreath for hanging.

6 To soften the effect, take small bunches of baby's breath and push them in between the ribbon wraps and the twigs. To complete the effect, mix some more baby's breath with the miniature roses and position them at the base of the heart. You can glue this spray in place, if you wish.

this point and bind the end of each with wire.

3 Bend each bundle around to form the pictured heart shape, then bind them to the end of the center column so that all three sections are held together securely.

4 Wrap the wire around four other points of the heart to hold the

Tuck small bunches of baby's breath into the ribbon

Sunshine

MATERIALS
1½ yds of 1" wide satin ribbon
florists' wire
foam ball
yellow everlasting flowers

INSTRUCTIONS

1 Cut 20" from the length of ribbon. Wire the two ends of the ribbon together with a long piece of wire. Push the wire through the ball of foam to the other side, then double it back on itself to secure it.

2 Cut the stems of the flowers very short and push them into the ball of foam until the whole ball is covered. Take care to pack the flowers in very tightly so that the foam does not show through. Keep the flower heads at the same height to maintain the spherical shape.

3 Make a double bow from the remaining ribbon, leaving almost no tail on the bow. Secure the bow with wire, leaving a tail of wire free. Push this tail of wire into the ball, between the two sides of the loop.

Above: The pomander, ready to hang
Left: Covering the ball with flowers

This is a pretty variation of the more common pomander made with an orange and cloves.

Sweet Dreaming (see page 54)

Sweet Dreaming

Wire the plants into large clumps

The muted tones and gentle shape of this pretty swag make it an ideal decoration for the bedroom.

MATERIALS
40" x 6" muslin
rosy sunray
oak leaves
leaf skeletons
pink wheat
fine spool wire
4 yds of 1" wide satin ribbon

INSTRUCTIONS

1 Separate the plants into large bunches and wire each one, leaving a long tail of wire.

2 Beginning at one end of the strip of organdy, gather the material softly into a bunch. Secure the gathering by wiring in a bunch of the rosy sunray. Repeat the process at regular intervals along the length of the fabric, gathering the organdy and wiring in a bunch of flowers each time.

3 To add contrast to the color scheme, add in some wired clumps of rust-colored oak leaves and some light-colored leaf skeletons. It is important to work with the garland lying flat, and to maintain the general shape while you work. This will enable you to see more clearly where the empty spots are and where the color contrasts are needed.

Wire the clumps of flowers to the organdy

Filling in the shape of the swag

Hang the swag over a headboard or drape it along the top of a large mirror, allowing the ribbons to trail downwards gracefully.

4 Next, wire the clumps of pink wheat in the folds of the material.

5 Make three double bows from the satin ribbon, securing each one with wire and leaving a long tail of wire as for the flowers. Wire the bows into the arrangement, using them to cover any wire that may be showing.

6 Cut the remaining ribbon in half, trimming the ends into a V-shape as shown. Wind the wire around the center of each length and use this wire to attach the ribbons to the swag, one at each end. Drape the swag over the headboard or between the bed posts of your bed.

To complete the picture, wire in the bows

MATERIALS

wreath base
green wreath wrap or florists' tape
¹/₂ yd floral cotton fabric
8 small foam balls
18 gauge stub wire
dried grasses
green love-lies-bleeding
white larkspur
small cones
broom blooms
1 ⁵/₈ yds of 1" wide satin ribbon

INSTRUCTIONS

1 Depending on the type of wreath base you choose, you may need to wrap it with green wreath wrap or florists' tape until it is completely covered. This is only necessary when you use a wreath base which tends to shed or fall apart.

Above: Making the frame
Right: The finished wreath

This lovely wreath, combining dried flowers, fabric decorations, seeds and grasses, is perfect for any time of the year. The flowers and other plants have been chosen to complement the colors in the fabric. Naturally, if your fabric has different colors, you should choose different flowers and plants.

2 Cut the floral fabric into squares that are big enough to cover the small foam balls. Cover each ball with a square of fabric, pulling the fabric quite taut and securing it with wire as shown. Leave long tails on the wire for attaching the balls to the wreath. Position the balls around the wreath, pushing the wires into the base to hold the balls in place.

3 Wire a few stems of green love-lies-bleeding together into small bunches, leaving a tail of wire as for the balls. Push the wired stems into the wreath base, keeping them close to the balls.

4 Wire clumps of white larkspur and insert those in the same way. The soft white of the flowers reflects the white in the fabric and adds a highlight to the arrangement. Next, wire three or four small cones together and place them "standing" upright around the wreath so they don't get lost among the other plants.

5 Soften the display by adding wired bunches of soft pink rabbit's tail grass throughout. The seeds of this grass shed very easily, so be careful not to overhandle them when wiring and inserting the grasses.

Above: Attaching the fabric-covered foam balls
Left: Wire in clumps of green love-lies-bleeding

6 The deep red color in the fabric is reflected in the broom flowers which are wired into small bunches to nestle among the other plants. Choose a dark red, rather than a bright one, to add depth to the display.

7 Tie ribbon bows and secure them with wire before inserting them close to the covered balls, trailing the streamer ends of the bows prettily over the edges of the arrangement.

Top: Wire in clumps of white larkspur
Above: Add satin bows for a finishing touch

59

Topiary

These delightfully shaped decorations, also called standards, are not really topiary but have that same sense of formal shaping. They have the great advantage of making a very dramatic impact while taking up very little space.

Your first step in making the tree is to choose the right container – one that suits the style of trimming you intend to use and the area in which it is to be placed. Bear in mind that the container will be filled with plaster of Paris, so if your chosen container is a valuable one or not entirely solid, you may prefer to use an inner and outer one. Plastic pots are ideal, but make sure you cover the drainage hole before pouring in the plaster.

The next step is to decide on the stem. A broom handle definitely will not do! Ideally, the stem should do more than just support the arrangement, it should add to it. Choose a stem with the right "weight" and character; sometimes two stems, entwined, can be very effective.

The pine cone tree shown here has all the elements of a harmonious arrangement: a very interesting, gnarled stem, a balance between the ball and the container, and an interesting use of dried materials contrasting with the green of the moss. If you want to place your tree in a basket, glue the nuts and pine cones in place first. Next, line the basket with plastic, center the stem in the basket and support it while you add the plaster of Paris. When the plaster has set, cut a little hollow into a ball of florists' foam and press it firmly onto the top of the stem.

Wrapping the ball with chicken wire gives it added strength. Wire the large pine cones individually and the smaller ones in groups, leaving a tail of wire. Press the wire tail into the ball, taking care to vary the size of the cones and to maintain the general shape. This one does not need to be a very formal shape.

Autumn Tree

This attractive tree uses cream, gold and various greens for a very natural coloring to contrast with the artificial shape. This is quite a large tree, ideal for narrow hallways, tight corners or by your front door.

MATERIALS

nails
*length of dowel or an attractive branch
    for the stem*
suitable pot or container
plaster of Paris
*strawflowers in yellow, cream and a
    few pink stems*
statice
baby's breath
yellow yarrow
*a variety of eucalyptus leaves in
    different shapes and colors*
foam ball
ornamental pot
tissue paper

INSTRUCTIONS

1 Hammer a few nails into one end of the dowel or branch for the stem. Sharpen the other end.

Above: Wire the flowers into small bunches
Opposite: The completed tree

2 Lay several sheets of newspaper in the bottom of the container, covering the drainage hole. Support the nailed end of the stem in the pot and surround it with wet plaster of Paris. Support the stem in an upright position until the plaster is set.

3 Push the foam ball firmly onto the sharpened end of the stem. Make sure it is centered.

4 Cut the flower and plant stems approximately 4" long. Wire the strawflowers individually and the other flowers into small bunches. The eucalyptus leaves may not need to be wired if they can be pushed into the foam without breaking.

5 Start to insert the trimmings into the foam ball, building up a circular perimeter to act as your guide for the shape. This will prevent you subsequently from having some bunches too far in or out of the circle. Remember, build up this perimeter shape from all angles – try to imagine you are creating a smooth round ball. Continue to press the trimmings into the ball until it is completely covered and no foam is visible.

6 Place the container with the tree into a larger ornamental pot. Scrunch up the tissue paper and press it into the top of the pot, covering the plaster. Cover the surface with baby's breath to conceal the tissue paper.

DAZZLING

chicken wire
moss
twigs
floral pins
raffia
foam ball
craft knife
orange and yellow everlasting flowers
blue larkspur
green love-lies-bleeding

INSTRUCTIONS

1 Choose an interestingly shaped branch to form the stem of the arrangement. Mix up plaster of Paris with water, enough to almost fill your container. Pour the plaster into the container and, while it is still wet, center the stem in the container. Support the stem until the plaster has started to set.

2 Make a ring of chicken wire: cut a rectangle slightly wider than two times the height of the container and

This ever-popular form of dried flower arrangement is not difficult to achieve, although it does require a little preparation. This little tree makes a delightful center-piece for your table. Make it with holly and berries instead of flowers for a very festive Christmas decoration.

MATERIALS
suitable small container for the base (a small plastic pot, with the hole covered, is ideal)
plaster of Paris
branch for the stem

Above: Prepare the pot, centering the stems in plaster
Right: Making the moss ring
Far right: The finished tree

slightly longer than the distance
around it. Fold the chicken wire in
half lengthwise and pack it with dry
moss. When it is fully packed, neatly
bend the raw edges over to close the
ring and join the ends.

3 Cut the twigs to the same length
and wire them around the moss,
using two floral pins for attaching each
twig. On the outside, cover the floral

pins by winding two lengths of raffia
around the twigs as shown.

4 Once the plaster has completely
set, place the container inside the
ring of moss and twigs. Scrape out the
center of the foam ball with a sharp
craft knife. Press the ball firmly onto
the wooden stem of the tree, making
sure it is held quite securely.

5 Wire the flowers into small
bunches, leaving a tail of wire at
least $1^1/_4$" long. Push the wired stems
into the foam ball, beginning with the
everlasting flowers to form the shape.
It is very important to build up a
smooth spherical shape that is the
same from all sides.

6 Next add the larkspur and love-
lies-bleeding, making sure they
do not distort the shape by protruding
from the arrangement.

7 Finish by tucking in some clumps
of moss to cover the plaster of
Paris and the chicken wire.

BEDSIDE TREE

MATERIALS
suitable branch for the stem
plaster of Paris
plastic pot
florists' foam ball
sharp craft knife
pink larkspur
22 gauge stub wire
small pink basket
moss

INSTRUCTIONS

1 Choose a plastic pot that fits neatly into the pink basket and does not quite reach the lip of the basket. Cover the drainage hole in the plastic pot and center the stem in the pot. Pour in the plaster of Paris and support the stem until the plaster has set.

2 Using the craft knife, cut a small hollow in the foam ball and firmly press it onto the top of the stem.

3 Separate the larkspur into florets and wire them in bunches of three or four, leaving a long tail of wire. Push the florets into the foam ball until it is entirely covered. Take care to maintain the lovely round shape.

4 Place the plastic pot inside the basket and cover the top with moss.

The impact of this little bedside tree comes from the unexpected way in which the flowers have been used. Instead of using tall stems of dried larkspur in the usual way to give height to an arrangement, the pink flowers have been packed densely to form this pretty tree.

The pretty pink tree for the bedroom

Special Touches

There are few rules when working with dried flowers and even they are flexible. Keep in mind restrictions about size, color balance, using complementary containers and flowers and so on – but do not be bound by them. Allow your creative imagination to flow freely and you can create arrangements that are unique and exciting.

This unusual design is defined by the white trellis, a common feature in many gardens. The trellis has been used as a blank artist's canvas where you can paint a picture with flowers. The "picture" may be quite small like this one, or very large, covering a whole wall with trellis work and including painted detail, archways and trompe l'oeil.

Once you have decided on the size and shape of your arrangement, choose your color scheme. In this arrangement, stems of larkspur, blue statice, everlastings, grains and grasses are wired into triple bunches, then wired onto the trellis and finally tied in place with raffia. Begin working at the top of the trellis, attaching each little bunch so that it covers the stems of the bunch above it. Bunches of lavender are wired in on their own. When you have finished wiring and tying in this way, tuck in some large clusters of love-in-a-mist to fill any gaps.

It is interesting to note that naturally colored flowers have been very successfully combined with dyed flowers. The sea holly has been dyed a steely blue, giving the stems a silvery appearance. Some of these stems, without heads, have also been scattered throughout the arrangement to maximize the effect of their lovely colors and forms.

POTPOURRI BASKET

MATERIALS
woven wicker cutlery tray
flat wicker tray
a selection of dried flower heads
potpourri
dried flower petals
tissue paper, moss or florists' foam

A dried flower decoration need not be a formal arrangement of flower stems arrayed in a vase or bowl. Sometimes, your raw materials can be a wonderfully decorative item on their own. This basket of potpourri is just such an arrangement.

INSTRUCTIONS

1 It is important that the basket looks lavish but you can cheat a little. The potpourri needs only to be about half an inch deep, just deep enough to conceal the filler beneath. Which filler you choose will depend on the shape and size of your container; tissue paper, moss and florists' foam are the most common ones. For a large container with awkward shapes such as this basket, tissue paper is ideal; foam would need to be cut to size and moss could be expensive. If you are using tissue paper, crumple it up tightly and pack it into the container, making sure that you reach right into the corners, so that you have a level base for the layer of petals and flowers.

2 Add your selection of potpourri, flowers and petals. Potpourri of petals has a wonderful scent but is not always very interesting in appearance. In this arrangement, the potpourri has been complemented with dried flowers, mixed in with the petals and decorating one corner of the basket. You can use flowers which are repeated in the potpourri or some which are completely different – just as you like.

3 Position your arrangement in the center of a table, away from open windows or doors where the potpourri could be blown about.

A delightful and informal tray of potpourri and flowers

A GRAND DISPLAY

Dried flower arrangements can vary in size from a tiny posy to a generously sized basket such as this.

Generally, large arrangements are best placed with plenty of space around them so they can be fully appreciated. However, large baskets make a wonderful filler for empty fireplaces during summer. If your kindling basket is a nice shape, why not use it for your flowers?

MATERIALS
large basket
an assortment of dyed and bleached
   everlastings
dyed teasels
bleached eucalyptus
dried ferns

INSTRUCTIONS

1 Make a chicken wire base to fit neatly inside the basket. It can be quite helpful to mound it up over the height of the basket rim.

2 Begin by laying in the rounded shape of the arrangement with the taller stems of teasels.

3 Wire the other materials into small bunches. Fill in with the eucalyptus, dried ferns and clumps of tiny everlastings, taking care to maintain the shape.

4 Use the graceful shape of the ferns to define the lower edge of the arrangement. Allow the ferns to drape downwards, covering the rim of the basket.

A generously sized basket houses a grand display

Large arrangements are very useful decorator items. Not only do they dress up a room, they can also camouflage its faults – such as an awkward empty corner.

WINTER FIREPLACE

The colors and textures of pine cones make them ideal for an autumn or winter decoration. The wreath uses similarly sized pine cones to give a very even appearance. You could vary the sizes, perhaps using larger cones around the bottom and graduating the size up to the smallest at the top.

MATERIALS
Trees
2 short, straight branches for stems
several short, straight branches, cut into tiny logs
nails and hammer
2 small cones of florists' foam
sharp craft knife

pine cones
22 gauge stub wire
Wreath
wire base
pine cones
22 gauge stub wire
glue gun

INSTRUCTIONS

For each tree

1 Nail the tiny logs into the shape pictured, securing the base of the stem in the center with glue and nails.

2 Cut a hollow in the center bottom of the foam cones. Firmly press the hollow onto the top of the stem.

3 Wire each pine cone with stub wire, leaving a long tail of wire.

Begin pushing the pine cones into the foam, beginning at the bottom and working round and round until the foam is covered and you reach the top.

For the wreath

1 Wire each pine cone with stub wire and then wire each cone to the wire base. It is a good idea to add a spot of glue where the cones touch one another to ensure that they stay in position.

2 When the glue is dry and you are happy with the arrangement, attach a wire loop to the back for hanging the wreath.

Arrangements of pine cones give a very dramatic effect on the mantelpiece

PRESSED FLOWERS

Pressing and arranging flowers is a delightful and inexpensive hobby. Homegrown flowers are free and you can make your own flower press quite simply, using very cheap materials (see page 17). How much you spend will depend largely on how you plan to mount and display your pressed flowers.

Ideally, flowers for pressing should be picked in the middle of the day when the dew has dried, and pressed without delay. Place small flowers face down on tissue paper, laid on top of blotting paper, before covering them with another sheet of tissue and blotting paper. Larger flowers can be placed directly on blotting paper. Multi-petal flowers, like carnations and roses, should be separated before pressing. Cut away thick stems and hard parts as well.

You will need very little in the way of special equipment when you first begin. You will be able to manage quite well with a couple of paintbrushes, some toothpicks, pencils, tweezers, sharp scissors, scalpel, white glue and some acid-free paper bags for storing your flowers. (The bags used to hold photographic negatives are ideal.)

It is important to handle pressed flowers with great care. Tiny flowers can be picked up with a needle tip or tweezers and moved around on the background with the aid of paintbrushes. Larger flowers can be picked up with slightly dampened fingers and tweezers.

To fix the flowers in place, use small amounts of the white glue. It is best to squeeze the glue onto an old plate, then use a toothpick to transfer a tiny dot of it to the flower. Larger flowers or sprays will need several dots of glue to secure them but take care that no glue shows on the front of the flowers.

When choosing the base for your pressed flowers, consider paper, fabric, wood, metal or plastic. Your background can be plain, colored or textured. Old fabrics, such as silks and satins, make a wonderful background for pressed flower pictures.

PRETTY AS A PICTURE

This delightful picture is not strictly an example of dried flowers, rather the result of pressing flowers, to give them that "just picked" look.

Left: First set down the outline of your shape
Below right: Begin to fill in with flowers covering the top of the stems
Below: Finally add a few pieces that droop

eye hooks and picture hanging wire
small hammer

MATERIALS
cream colored silk for the background
selection of grasses and foliage for the outline
an assortment of pressed flowers
sharp craft knife
tweezers
paintbrush
white glue
toothpicks
batting
suitable frame with glass and back panel insert
brads

INSTRUCTIONS

1 Take the back off your frame. Cut the silk to the same size as the panel insert. Cut a piece of batting the same size. Lay the panel insert on a flat surface with the batting and then the silk on top.

2 Using the tweezers to position the floral elements and the paintbrush

or toothpicks to apply the glue, begin to form your picture, starting with the outline and the short stems at the base.

3 Add the pressed flowers, working from the top of the picture with the palest colors. Work down the sides, filling in the outline as you go and layering flowers to give depth to the picture. Start adding in the stronger-colored flowers, taking care to cover the tops of the stems. Finally, add some flowers that droop down.

4 Use a dry paintbrush to sweep away any loose particles. Carefully lay the cleaned glass over the picture, then lay the frame on top. Turn the picture over and lay it on a soft surface. Fix the backing into place by hammering in the brads. Seal around the edges of the backing with masking tape stuck over the brad heads. Attach two eye hooks and a cord for hanging your picture.

The framed picture

The container is as important as the arrangement. Filling this large, glass vase with moss gives the arrangement a very unusual appeal.